Half Moons and Falling Stars

All best wishes!

Anna Di Bella

BOOKS BY ANNA DI BELLA

I WILL NOT NAME YOU
THE WARMTH OF PRESENCE

Half Moons
and
Falling Stars

by

Anna Di Bella

Cover Watercolor Art
Phyllis Rutigliano

FORE ANGELS PRESS

ISBN 09658920-2-6

Published by
FORE ANGELS PRESS
267 Woodbury Road
Huntington, New York 11743

Acknowledgements

Creations, Elf, Eve's Legacy, Goodfoot, Catskill Mountain Region *Guide, The Literary Review* (Performance Poets), *The Long Islander, Long Island Quarterly, Pegasus, Xanadu.*

Some prizewinning poems in this collection have been published or reprinted by Composers, Authors, Artists of America, Inc. and The National League of American Pen Women, Inc. The PEN WOMAN.

The author thanks Louis P. Di Bella, Maria E. Kiley, Tatiana Baque, Donald T. Kiley, Jr., Beverly Beyer, Joyce Bloch, Jeff Bohr, Tracie Herring and those friends who have so much inspired me.

Contents

For my husband Louis, fire and ice,
and the love of my life
and our son, John, a loving paradox.

Half Moons and Falling Stars

"I am a woman searching
for my savagery
even if it's doomed."
June Jordan

Dialogue in the Woods
(After Sandro Chia)

Let us dialogue in these woods
under the eaves of trees
where only leaves can bend to hear.

Let our words lend symmetry
to these moments shared
in closed communion.

Let us forget our frailties
and new frontiers for now
and let us delay the emptiness

when deprived each of the other,
no affections will be easily enjoyed.
Do know the day will come

when we will not lie languishing
under the same blue sky
or look to one another for surprise.

Twilight

                The moon sings blue,
sends sounds of crescent forms across
across the grey wood deck and what
was stillness of a sudden becomes
becomes white flares breaking
breaking into the calm center of
every sense and sentiment we have ever
known together or alone: we who are
so strangely sorry sorry for all
we have and have not done.
Listen as the magic moon plays tunes
for the foolish fortune seekers we are
whimpering for fear of what we still may lose
though surely even the unspangled skies
would weep cold tears for us
would send the rains to wipe away
what dust remains shrouding our warm and waiting graves
because the skies know too
how much we both have lost. Enough.

On Waiting

When you wait for someone
for a minute, or an hour, or a day,
it is like suffering the waiting
of a new moon. How you wish
you could be elsewhere with
someone waiting for you.

And if you wait in the rain
every drop is like a tear
flooding the pathways to escape;
and how self conscious you become,
your hands sweaty and your brow
a little moist from make-believing
that the wait is over and
that he or she or they will come
and you are not unworthy
for the wait.

Such Things Are

Walking to the river,
I watch the shore line bend
to meet the tide.
Only the natural stride
of slave to master,
rendering obedience
and surrender.

Walking to the river,
I watch the shore line bend
and move aside.
Myself sliding
into the rhythm
of the testing tide.

Waking to the White Ways

And then the rain came,
imperceptible at first,
soft and steady,
glazing the roadways
in silver sheen,
cross-stitching the houseplot grasses
with crisp embroidery,
leaving behind a subtle limpid breeze,
everything clean and clear.
There seemed no reason now
to leave the city,
but for the persistent memory
of a former drought
in this very place.

Or was it another?

Assignation

When we meet and you toss a pale green eye,
I know it for what it is.
You are not here.
You have brought your shadow
to negotiate our pleasure.
But since this is no meeting of the minds,
I abdicate,
toss back a brown sling of recognition,
a feigned arrow of remorse
and give you nothing.

Aftermath

Whenever the rivers flood,
the rages rise
above the contours
of a mind's discretion.
And soon the heart beats fast,
the blood curls cool,
and logic lurks defenseless
in the shadows.

Whenever the rivers flood,
the rages rise.
How do we quell
the breaking of the tides?

There is Intimacy in the Substance
of Found Space

The woods are thick,
twigs beat at our ankles,
branches clutch at our hair,
Yet, we see no reason to turn back.

The path ahead seems clear
in spite of brambles.
But as we walk the density of day,
when green casts shadows
in an overlay of foam,
we find ourselves tightpressed
against each other,
and we cannot breathe
the casual easy breaths
we shared in early dawn.

There are no spoken words.

We catch our thoughts as fireflies
and then extinguish them . . .
each of us afraid to invade
this newfound space
we have found
on mutual ground.

On Keeping An Open Window
or Conspiracy

By some conspiracy, the chilly dawns
and anxious morning winds
draw you closer to me
or I to you,
when I have pulled away
or you have pushed me off.
In spite of wills
and unwillingness,
mercurial messages conspire
to near us one to another:
cold feet and circling toes
find their easy comfort,
fetal positions exchange
for causal slips and slides:
four arms, four legs,
all body parts alert to accept
what last night's hearth fire
could not induce: submission.

A New Geometry

The thrust of granite rockhills
spears clear sky
and bluing clouds ghost
the sloping snow,
returning us to other places,
spaces where triangles met
and chosen corners of mist
squared away our linear existence,
so that in circles we might protract
a new geometry of stillness,
so that we need not dive
to stir the greying waters.

As the Foxes Leave Caumsett Park

Let the foxes find
their urban haunts.
Let them approach
our driven streets.
They only come to know
what we have done
to pristine places
where they dwelled.
And when they see,
believe . . .
they will retreat,
wanting no more of us.
You need not be afraid.
They will not stay.

Perennial

I dwell in an experiential place
where strangely flowers bloom,
but then, too soon, they die
from lack of lusterlife.
I cast no blame on cold environment,
rely on faith and past which speaks
of seeds and a rebirth of sorts.

When flowers sweet regenerate
I come to understand:
there is a preordained
propelling plan.

Looking Skyward

Skies white and clarifying
slice through the maze of mind,
and, unmindful of skyglare
this mid-March day,
I script my own drama,
a sweeping closure
and a calm redemption,
relenting now to mind's mercy,
its promise of an early spring
and you returned to me.

Laired Sleep

All night I listen to the lions roar,
and though I know there are none,
in my heart I hear them solemnly.
And as the grasses grow,
they also grow - taller, taller -
as large as granite monuments,
　　　unhoofed stone
　　　looming above the land.

All night I listen to the lions roar,
and as I listen
learn;
there is no sound
　　　but ragings in my heart.

So Be It: Caves are Bare

so it is that caves are bare
cavernous empty spaces
dismal and forlorn

so it is that every prayer
uttered in Any Place
is wingless borne

so it is that these swan fare
oblivious of winter waste
full feathered and unshorn
　　　　so it is

17

To All Who Would Rebel

All things bend
to the curve of the sun,
lean to its arc,
learn the scathing flash
of flame burning to ash.
All who rebel,
who beckon a blanched crested moon,
learn and too well
that the first primal frost
seared as it quelled.
And so it is
that all things bend
to the curve of the sun.

The Color of Silence

The moon is full tonight and luminous,
chalk-white in contradiction, in a sky
of indigo that silhouettes your face.
The tides are turned by such a moon as this
as are my passions turned to tenderness
when starless canopy is not abyss.
The moon is full tonight and luminous.

At the Side of a Banshee

And have you settled yet
into that netherworld
where heaven and the purgatories
set by the same sun?

You woke by startle
to jazzrock,
fell asleep to rolling drums.
Your dayworld was vibrato.
Ministering dark angels
pitched their tents at your feet,
strumming disquietingly deep.
How could you find comfort
in some objective slumberland?

You have found your place
at the side of banshee,
wailing at some orb.
There are other stars
and other moons and suns.
I suspect you will know them now
One to One.

Quartet on Grief

My grief is unconventional.
It won't follow rules or ritual.
It protests long laments.
And equally subdued silences.

My grief is restless.
It won't sleep or let sleep.
Pulling the covers over it,
only makes it squirm;
and swaddling doesn't work.
My grief has learned
to undo the pins.

My grief is like a fox
approaching city streets.
It is proud and primitive,
and it is afraid of traffic.

My grief wants friends.
It keeps shaking hands
with strangers.

.

Papá, Ti Vedo Dapertutto
(Papa, I See You Everywhere)

On weekday mornings
you never left the house
without white shirt and tie,
the invincible immigrant
a slice above them all.
You held your head up high,
a man six feet and more,
whose citizenship papers read:
five feet, eight inches.
But then, weren't our men
supposed to be short and swarthy?
You never left without a kiss,
"Ení, vieni qui."
That kiss cautioned me to be a good girl.
"Farli vedere." Let them see who you are,
who we are. I never left the house
without taking you with me
and mama too who in my head
always wore wide black tulle hats
and shoes so Euròpean, so elegant,
she always stood ten feet above me.
How could I be my mother,
or the woman you wanted me to be:
a doctor, a lawyer . . . o, what did you expect?
I wanted to be Veronica Lake, Amelia Earhart,
a Buddhist priest, a poet.

The Ways of the Netherworld

When my mother died,
I knew the angels had stolen her,
just as we were getting acquainted.
They were jealous.
There is no accounting for pettiness.

When my father was dying,
I knew the devils were coming for me.
I could hear them screaming
beneath the bedcovers.
As I shaved him, I heard him rasping,
negotiating my future, and
when his hands chilled blue
against white sheets,
I knew he had made a deal
to go in my stead.
Even dead he is paving my way.

This Mother Did Not Give Her Lamb

Even if I gave my blood for you
or a pound of flesh,
I could not barter
for you are beyond the place
where deals are made;
and if by some small chance
I could make the trade,
it would be my pawned disgrace.
Because I do not want you
for the world
but for my grace.
And, there can be no reason
at this my mourning place.

Through My Most Grievous Fault

This is no stranger at your grave
tossing dark roses.
Each petal is a platelet
borne of her marrow,
but she feels no loss
as she bleeds bouquets.
For she is long dead
and the ghost she grooms
to strew these roses
is her shadowform.
You need not be afraid.
The mother you knew
is buried in bare ground
alongside you.
This is no stranger at your grave.

Beyond Naples, April, 1997

The hills are human
in this part of the world,
haunched like benevolent relatives
leaning over the family ruins.
Early morning, they hover protectively,
keeping the spying sun out of the eyes
of unsuspecting tourists
mesmerized by sunglazed scenery.

The sky, a pale porcelain blue,
surrounds a veil of green,
and the earth, rich brown,
catches glints of yellow afternoons.
Behind the sloping, dormered hills,
sheep still graze, and faded farm children
faze out dreams of buried books,
and of life burning in tall, cathedraled cities.

Hidden by sheltering hills,
the children work the harrowed fields,
raking under and over the growing evergreens,
and when the olives are ripe,
like small machines they unflesh the pits,
churn the virgin fruit, watch the liquid spill
into big black barrels

and fill themselves with chartreuse dreams
of sweet new oil on fresh baked bread
and nana's pasta pies at Eastertime.

The cities are miles and miles away,
and they hear there's no work anyway,
and the hills are human
in this part of the world,
sending down cool breezes in the early evenings.
And the tourists come-- again and again
to be spellbound by the scenery,
and they straddle away with liter tins
of extra virgin olive oil
to heighten the taste of city salads
of endive and arugula.

Beyond Naples, when schoolbuses come
it is time for play. It is always time for play,
as they bury books in their chartreuse dreams.

Parable: The First Good Friday

From here to where
must this poor beggar go
to keep his alms.
"Move," you told him,
and he walked and walked
past the cemeteries where the dead
are buried in unconsecrated ground.

Because you asked him,
he shook his tired feet
of the old dry leather and is barefoot now.
He stands a man alone,
prepared for absolution.
At the mercy of what or whom?
Do you want him to wear brown beggar's smock?

Do you want him to kneel
before the throngs gathered here?
Restart his journey with an unfilled sack?
Let him go. Bless his bounty
and let him go.

This is no ordinary day.
Look, the skies are heavy.
Soon the rain will fall.
There are many strangers in the square.
Let him go. No one will know.

Leading Me On

I cannot understand that light
that lies behind the vining tree.
It shines in circles dim and dark
that move away, away from me.

The hollow is a shallow grave.
I never dropped into its depth,
but I remember who rests there,
and now the light is my own death.

On Relinquishing Past

The memory of your flesh
and his and hers
palpates on my fingertips
as I feel your pulsebeats
waning to my touch
which has always been sensitive
to the lines of blood:
but bleeding now to a new line,
running off to a new wild way.

I search for freedom now
from memories impeding flight
to newer, more natural skies
screaming crimson-yellow,
Munchian canvases, woeful but bold,
devoid of old melancholies
and hot, hot griefs.
Let me be, I say.
Let me be Lord of my place.

Waiting for an April Sun

The end of March
precludes mention
of February storms
stampeding the deckscreens.
We look to spring and crocuses
budding along the perimeters
of the garden highhedges
over which we peered
all those weary days
when we sought to find
some sturdy blooms.

One morning while you slept,
I broke the barricades.
Scratching the hard earth,
I cradled the buried bulbs,
screaming for yellow.
When you awoke, you spoke
of strange ancestral sounds.
I answered with cemetery silence.
My fingers still ached.

Morning with Arthur

This is a morning I have never known:
Not with bluegreen, oleandered hills.
What a spook of a morning:
you,
lifting this yellow doubled eye
from its night grief.

Seagull Motive
After a Painting by Arthur Dove

The seagull had a motive,
morsels of fishchips.
He squealed and I
relented. It hardly mattered
(the giving up of fried cod)
until I saw your oil
and realized
his white feathered frame
harbored a dark hunger.

One Way Conversation

At the beginning we sang with the dolphins,
heaved our chests to their joyful swoops,
praised opal skies with willful water dances.
How is it that now we hear no music?
That we walk in stiff conceit?
Turn shy eyes away from sky and song?
Why this unseasoned waning?
Did it come upon us quick and fast
as some marauder seeking easy plunder?
Or did we ourselves silently surrender,
looking away from palisades of sky,
mimicking the empty moon with no reply?

From That Port to This

How can it be? There is no language between us
to bridge the rifts or galvanize the gaps.
At odds with ourselves and with each other,
the gods wage battle on our behalf.
But we are indifferent, we are indifferent.
Once, when we warred, we paid reparations,
vowed to amend and close the widening ranks.
Now there are no such maneuverings.
The rule books have been lost at sea.
This is, perhaps, a new kind of war.

South of Myself

I am south of myself these days.
How have I traveled so far
to this hot spot
where my sun blisters?
Why have I traveled so far
when steelcold is my mettle?

Between the Pews

On the first day I was to take
the body of Christ, I fainted.
It was the thought of drinking blood
that felled me.

I was at eight, am now, carnivorous,
but to be a drinker of blood,
red and vital, was too much
even for me who intended
her confirmation name to be
Veronica, Veronica not of the magic veil -
Veronica, Veronica Lake.

"Anna, Anna, wake up,
Father is waiting."
My mouth hymns, "Let him wait, Sister."
My lips say, "I am dizzy.
Let me go last, Sister, please."
And when I reach the altar,
surrounded by clouds of white,
I see only the wafer and
I cry. I cry for joy,
and Sister says,
This is one of the happiest days of your life."
"Yes," I say. "Yes, Sister."

Perimeters of Time

These are the hours
of our mutual lament.

Punctuated by the pain
of sentenced grief

we move. . . move slowly
along perimeters of time,

watching the blossoms grow,
the seagulls fly,

the landscapes change,
as landscapes will,

to satisfy the seasons.
We pray to be ensnared,

as in a spider's web,
luminated by glare

of lamp and moon,
pray to hang limply there

to wait for that brief moment
of final benediction,

and when it comes,
we will be prepared.

At the Gate

If I can find you
I will resurrect you,
but you are invisible.
You have traveled beyond,
in spite of foolish stories you have told:
"I will be with you always."
"At your side - young or old."
"I will be there. I am. I am."

You are not, you know.
You are gone. You are behind
the primroses at the gate,
pulling hydrangeas from their branches,
hiding near the hemlocks.
How can I resurrect you
if you play at the changes of the wonderful seasons,
in places where I cannot touch you
or feel your soft flesh
inaccessible for the fleeting.

On Caravans of Pain

When I was looking to die
landscapes became greener still
and sitting at my side a reel physician
framed my lifespace
connecting configurations:
(the long shots were too close
and the close-ups seemed
dark distances away.)
Caravans of white-robed angels
drifted by impatiently;
and everything disfigured
came to me figuratively perfect
so that I sought none else.
And so it was that when
I was looking to die
the death-bolt detonated.
And as if at some-old-picture-show,
the actors moved to horizon,
and they were not dead.
In fact, the last frame read
"The Beginning."

Dear Piet

How good to know
dear Piet
that you flaked flowers
skull types
and faceless orbs
and crucificial
heart-lit
charcoaled blue
botanicals.

Caught between grids
between
stiletto scaffolding
and spine design
there was Piet
[after all]
a thin thin line
between
that architecture
      and
your very own.

O, Imperfectly Understood Are You
After An Early Mondrian Painting

Your tree is grey;
mine is purpleshadowed,
hides deep dark scars:
not the ordinary scars
of ruptured bark,
a new kind - -
slit silvered marks
that bleed not sap
but the red hot blood
of wide white wounds.
I envy your grey tree:
web-like branches splayed
in stark abstraction.
I envy your grey tree.
It has no flesh.

All Fleshless Trees Tease Memories

And when the birch peeled
its white skin
I thought I saw his skeleton
standing there, and he,
shaking his strong bone finger
at me, shaking my rapt attention.

And all the while I thought:
Why did he shed his skin?
Those fingers fine as flint.
Why did he shed his skin?
Without the full of flesh,
he looms so thin.

Brushfire Dream

White seagulls stain a sunblazed sky
and flying near, a swarm of birds,
some black, some blue,
inkspot like leaves

and then disband and rupture fire.
A span of sudden open wings
embraces sky and gulls and birds,
usurps the stage. And all is white.

A stroke of death, or stroke of life?

Oblique

A herd gatherer, you summon your sheep.
They bleat. You find a comfort zone,
sawed grasses, a sprawling hill.
You lie with them, examining the stars,
small blistering bursts flaring obsidian.
Your sheep belong to you. They are faithful.
Whatever covenant is made is made in faith.
Your staff is their reward.
Sheared of the wool they give and more,
they follow where you lead.
The thin night air you breathe
becomes a sheath . . . protection.
You sing deep desert songs. They imitate.
They learn your melodies, maraud the fields.

Half Moons and Falling Stars

If you told me you could read the stars, it would be enough for me, my eyes glazed and staring, the sky blatantly blue and spilling as from some old inkwell. It would be enough if you told me you understood my hysterical chants through half moons and falling stars, understood my shrill night bleats, - - a small lamb seeking its shepherd. But you sit stone-faced, no smiling Buddha. You sit stone-faced reading me, and I undecipherable. You can not read the stars and you can not read me, and I so needy of legibility let my silk scarves fall wherever they will - - casting shadows against opaque.

Numbered Days of Half Prayer

So many rainfalls have caught us
beneath so many bruised branches.
We have forgotten now
more than we can remember:
so many words thrashed
east and west,
north and south.
O, what will we take with us?
The flow of rain?
Its staining dark?
The memorized pink dawns?
The bluing nights?
O, what will we take with us?
Please let it be the green parade
of land and sea that freed us
from too many inner storms
and too many somber shadows.

Prepared for Shards

I hunted God one day.
But he would have no part of me.
He sent me off instead
To find some other prey
In the forested fields
He had grassed with sparrows.
It was a wasteful chase.
I found no life
To fall upon my sword.
But I learned one lesson well.
If you would hunt,
Be master of the game.
And be prepared yourself
To be its prey,
Or be undone for lack of enemy.

No Shadow World
A Sonnet for Edwin Ver Becke

There is bold beauty in the inner eye
That sees beyond the span of time and space,
And void of reason reaches out to grace
A wanting world and never asks it why.
Yes, brittle branches break and lilacs die,
And cyclamen change color, lose their face,
Submit and perish at the season's pace,
And every rose that blooms broods a goodbye.
Yet heart pleads passionate and stirs wildfire,
Enflames the vision and reclaims the light
Burning within, refuses to expire
That blazing torch of luminating sight.
A tortured beauty sparks the inner eye,
Transfixing earth, four winds, and sea and sky.

To Make Good Use of Eden

Green mountains stretch below a purpled sky
That canopies brown earth, protecting land,
Dispersing thunderbolts white lightning high,
Above a disemboweled cratered sand.
No respite here though heavens release a crown:
Stone stars that spill from planets still unnamed,
To luminate a universe unbound
Where suns and moons and dreams lie dark, untamed.
A whirling world unconjured, of a kind
That chronicles a narrative untold,
A spinning history that splinters mind,
And then lets loose hot atoms to burn cold.
So flares our thirst to learn how Is began.
We quench by myth incendiary plan.

Analogy

A heron occupies a limb.
A branch accommodates
the teeter legs.

A mind exfoliates
untethered words
in mock apology.

Some balance is restored
in tree and universe.

Flirtation

Is this a gathering of mockingbirds
lurking in the hightrees?
We don't recognize their calls,
those calls that mimic other trillers.
When I whisper prose poems under my breath,
I imitate their rhythms and their bold wild calls.
Tell me, are these mockingbirds at all?

You know how circumspect we are,
how reverent and fearful of the obscure.
And yet, the songs of the unidentified can lure.

Words Overheard: Spoken by the Woman Charged With Adultery

Where have you gone,
my brother, my lover, my friend?
Where have you gone?

The temple is cold,
and the stones strike bold.
Where have you gone?

When we lay in the field,
your body would shield me
from harm.
Now where have you gone,
my brother, my lover, my friend?

They unplaited my hair,
and some stripped me bare.
When I looked to the crowd,
I thought you were there.
Was I wrong?

Where have you gone
my brother, my lover, my friend?
When will it end?

Note to a Nighttime Lover

Don't be afraid
o, please don't be afraid
I did not mean
to stir you
sound awake,
I only meant to touch
and then to take
that which you,
startled,
might then
willing
give.

So Love Must Be

How quick to quell the upsurge
Expel it from the heart
How quick I am denying it
As some unstaged upstart
How quick I am dispelling
The rage you spat at me
The venom that so vilified
Is quashed from memory.

Still Life or Life Still

I am a spendthrift
and you are thrifty.
Going to market
with you
is not fun for me.
Whoever heard
of coming home
with full pockets
and a basket
half empty.
Going to market
with you
is not fun
for me.

Negotiations Notwithstanding

I like your silences,
procrastinated moments of anticipation
as you anxiously wait for a flash flood of words
cascading.
Or am I mistaken.
Do you prefer a silent response
to your attenuated observations?
Do you prefer:
my eyes cast downward,
my chin hugging my chest,
no utterance at all?
Answer me. I need for you to answer me.

Wordspills

If I could, wanting to, stop my mouth
from running off like a faulty faucet,
I would.
If I could, like a word plumber might,
fix the leak, put the washers in,
I would.
But the maelstrom is unleashed, courses,
a barreling overflow flooding the emptiness,
disrupting everything around as any waterspill.
I am so ashamed.
After the deluge,
as water whirls,
I weep the widow's wail
as all alone she fondles what is lost.

Contacts

I see you with my eyes closed,
through the brilliant fires
of uncataracted remembrances.
How do you see me?

Not at all.

Not for a Minute

I cannot care
or dare
to be
the key
that pries the door
to your
dark heart,
nor start
the fire to burn,
nor learn
to play
your way.

A minute is sixty seconds. It is also a twelve line poem
following a syllable count and a rhyme scheme as above.

On Transformation

These graying walls are played upon by light
That filters through this dappled pane of glass.
The shifting shadows cast are birds in flight,
Leaving their nesting birch and flying fast
To some abandoned nest of seasons past.

And is it so with those who leave this plane,
Take fast their flight, minds resolute and clear,
Whose shadows are paled skies and summer rain,
Swift streams of sun, spotsplintering the pane,
Blinding remembrances of life aflame?

Looking for Light

There are no birds
in this moonsleeping sky.
No flutter and no fuss,
no promise of tomorrow.
It is providential
that you do not look up
with hope and expectation.
Whatever push and pull there is
in this proofed canvas,
you too can conjure
with your plaintive eye.

Middlepath

You have moved into a silent spring,
into a red autumn of the blasted tree
where you sing sutras to ancient Buddhist saints
the Worthy Ones who languish from neglect.

You need no mattresses of layered green,
no fickle frost, no sheltering snow.
Unseasoned actor, you need no backdrop now.
You are found. You have found the middlepath.

Marshes by Daylight

If I had listened to the winds,
they might have brought me messages
of your whereabouts.

But I, perverse as any solitary heron,
waded through the waters
looking for you.

You were not there. I found instead
remnants of other lives:
old belts, old tires,
and even one old workboot,
a nest for spiders.
No poetry. No you.

But I was satisfied,
seeing that the spiders
were floating still,
seeing that the spiders
        are
floating still.

More or Less

There are too many moons
on this planet.
And all of them too round,
too bright, too synchronized;
too many frail five-pointed stars
that shine unbrightly
in this greying sky
interrupted by indigo dreams
exploding to fire - orange -
    and blue -
There are too many suns
to parch this planet.
And can it be,
there are too many planets
        too?

We Have a Memory of Light

The overhang of sky
looms above the stippled trees.
When will the moon visit?

Between the Lines

If I crawl into one of your poems,
will you recognize me,
slipping through the shadow lines?
Will you recognize me
tripping over the green toed citizens
of Bosnia or Rawanda?
Will you recognize me sweating blood
in my black beret, red cape and
Capuchin-brown crushed slippers?
Will you recognize me
in my hangman's noose?

Hold My Inheritance

A single corpse can be
a mass grave,
dismembered particles,
a part of the atomic structure
that defines indifference,
disputes the fallacy
of human love.
How subject to dismal
uncertainties we are.
The knowing of ourselves.
The unknowing of ourselves.
Don't look at graveheaps
in warfields or in your memories
expecting absolution
for the kindness
in your weeping eyes.
You are part
of the atomic structure
that defines indifference,
protective as you are
of your own being.

A Promise

Take me to some other place
where olives fall from crippled trees
standing rigid in the groves.
Take me as I was, not am
and I will let you see that part of me
I most am now.

For us now the end is near,
and if we leave behind vehement words
and wasted wishes, we will never find
the sweet succulent berries we rolled over
our blistered tongues in prayer.
How could we? How could we?

Since this is so, take me to some other place,
where paths are thick with roping vines.
Together, we can unsift the earth,
retrieve the waters from fevered wells
and know the pungent oils of life again.
Together we can. I promise you.

Birth

A wild wind, a blistering mountain breath
spits us out, sprawls us
against a rock hard vastness.

We feel a splintering of bone
losing its frame of reference.
We crawl into private cells
of nothingness.
Left in the void is mind
disappropriated,
mind memorizing
an ancient code
calligraphied in neglect.

On Figs and Marriage

There you are smiling
from the color slide,
delicious mouth wide open
flashing the celluloid.

Like fig trees bulbing,
vying for my attention,
you have seduced me
so many times
with summer promises.

You need not be concerned.
Come cold, I will blanket you,
cocoon you for my pleasure,
come spring, come summer
come fall,
the world with you is photogenic.

This Midnight Clear

Tired of incandescent lights
whirling my brain,
I give myself
to dark swirling shadow corners.
The moon, evasive,
slights me,
scathes all the days
of our together.
Close your eyes and
feel forever now
this midnight clear.

On a Journey to Opaque

There are misty mornings such as this
when thin thin fog greyshrouds
the trees around me
and they stand as strong spine ghosts
and the concrete curls beneath my feet
and the tires of my leased car slip from me
and the steering wheel is warped
and rusted still, but I turn turn
turn it and it takes me where I should be
away to some other place.

Everything so so strange
on such misty mornings as this
when the thin thin fog greyshrouds me
and nothing is as it should be
but everything is just
and ashen ghosts protect me
from myself.

". . . A Slant of Light"
Emily Dickinson

How obscure we are this spring.
There is no telling of ourselves
or the forsythia
which come so late
and so pale yellow.

In other springs
the garden grasses grew
in velvet patches
and everything seemed anxious
to break through.

Not so this year which I have named,
" The year the earth changed."

As Ashes Smolder

The mind will cry for vengeance,
seething white heat.
Taking course without remorse,
deadening as it sears.
Revenge is clear and clarifying:
cremates,
incinerates.
The mind will cry for vengeance.
Ashes smoldering still burn.

Confession

I take blame here but to tell the truth
indifference is not my game.
I rage with fire in every limb
until I extinguish myself
and smoke down to ashes.
Beneath I burn, burn, burn.
I have never understood
your passion for dark silences.
They are never silences of submission
and there is never any shame.

Tic-Tac-Toe

Square by square I ungame you,
probing your makeshift boundaries.
Here and there a wry smile,
a jagged reminder of
old memories I hold
of a summer long ago.

You stare me down
as you throw your weight around.
I turn away and fidget with my keys.
Your anger vibrates.
It has its own rhythm,
its own momentum.

I am immobilized.
But there will be another time.
Global wars are made like this.

Passions Reflected

How many times have I touched you, felt you rise beneath my feeling fingers? So many times we cannot count, lost as we are in the fragile forgetfulness of old lovers.

As many times, surely, we have carelessly probed each other, appeased our appetites, not out of love or lust, but out of a primitive need to be. And not let be.

Forgiveness

It is not about flowers
and cryptic notes.
It is about the wringing of hands
under the table,
the gritting of teeth,
the choking and the spitting up
of unmasticated meat,
the smashing of fine porcelain,
and the giving in to wrath.
And it is about your need one day
to ask this of another.
It is not about flowers
and cryptic notes.

The Politics of Surrender

We are ripped apart,
torn from our own cloth,
no ordinary fabric.
They tried to stitch us together
so that we might keep up appearances,
but it was no use. No use at all.
The stretching had stripped the seams,
and it seemed unkind not to give way,
not to give in to the menders
for whom there could be no peace
had there been no rending.
We surrender.

There is Nothing to Be Known
of What is Now

All is preserved in monotonic memory.
Sounds of the moments fade, are juxtaposed
against the marbled memories of toneless time
and dark, stark places perceived as soundless now.

We strive to waken stifled harmonies;
seek to hallucinate; to conjure colors;
to bring about a vibrating change;
to create an ongoing permanence
like ocean waves perpetuating new waves.

And now and then we search to futurize,
but always fall into a vapored haze.
There is nothing to be known of what is now.
Sounds of these moments fade, are juxtaposed.

No need to seek them out. We hold them safe.

On Suspending Time

Lying in chartreuse fields,
eyes open to citrus skies above,
we are mesmerized by everything beyond,
knowing our days seasoned by this green
are not our own, belonging as they do
to time churning, rewording our universe
in idioms foreign to us as we claim
the incandescence of another spring.
Lying in chartreuse fields, eyes closed,
we are mesmerized by everything still possible.

For My Great Aunt

Vincenza placed ripe fruit
in bowl and basket
and tended to their care.
"Non si sa chi verrá."
"You never know
who will drop in."
We all laughed
at the primping
and the polishing
of summer fruit,
not knowing then
that this small chore
was part of her charade.
We never listened and
we never heard
the trembling of her wings.

A Poem for Jeanette Who Makes Birdsounds

I hardly know the earth.
The names of trees and flowers are enigma.
Maps evade me. I have no sense of space.
Know no mountains by their names.
Hills and peaks for me are symbols
Rising and falling. Rising and falling.
The sky, obsidian: attracts me.
Mauve: distracts me.
Grey: contracts my vision
And I seek for stars hiding
Or gliding past: false points of light.

I am mesmerized by everything you know:
How you see seeds sprout, call them by name,
How you are intimate with stones,
Hold small crystals in your hand,
Seducing them to splinter or to resist your touch.
But most of all, I am in awe
When you recognize the tracks of rat or fox.

Manblood

There is a bond between fathers and sons
evasive as an unsolicited breath,
a small death to singleness.
Genetic or not, the cells are circumscribed.
Continual, unclear, ambiguous but real
as firebranded mark.
No geographic break,
no fall from grace,
no shedding of the skin, nothing,
not even the closing of a grave,
unfuses the bond engraved
in manblood.

A Note to My Son

Males, sons, are their fathers' heirs,
decried to carry names,
honed histories and anecdotes:
the sum of heritage
for grandsons of immigrants.

But I am the storyteller,
and my child, midway in cycle,
must learn to listen to the winds
and whispers of stories stretched
over oceans, over decades of
emotional debris and a sea,
stories stretched to siphon
family feuds and the crude remnants
of family bones. . . .

He must learn to listen,
ears pared and slate grey eyes prepared,
or he will lose generations
of socio-genetic pool.
I must tell him:
Males, sons, are their fathers' heirs.
But I am the storyteller.

Factored to My Minimum

"How do you do it," I hear you say.
I answer, "Well, my head is all at play."
The answer deep within is dark as hell.
When the chimes sound, I don't hear the bell.

This Place of Mind

A place of mine
where jeweled words
like pebbles
line the mind.

A place of mine
where hills shake stars
like lava bolts
of shine.

A place of mine
where solitude
and silence
spill as wine.

A place of mine
where unequivocally
I am delivered
all pulp, no rind.

Even as the Skies Wane

There is no ocean here:
only crisp Bay waters
brazenly blue.
Soon the boats will chop the calm,
stirring everything beneath.
But I will know it is not,
having memorized
the breakings
of those loud green summers
when the tides axed wild.

*And it will seem like ocean
that we bequeath.*

90

The Rendering

A round and fired globe is sun,
that overtakes the bland blue sky,
and razes every tranquil plane.
Nothing can be the same again.

"Do Not Confuse Impedance
    With Impediment"
                        Oxford American Dictionary

There is a total resistance here,
an impediment to the alternating flow.
Electricity can not be charged.
The circuit is dead.
Whatever happened to the current,
immediacy retained?
Whatever happened
to those bouts of intimacy
rigorously sustained
by each and both
in subdued submission?

Go to the dictionary, friend.
Do not confuse impedance
with impediment.

Jigger - Plus One

You measure
passion
in jiggerfuls,
you the two-sided
one
who measures
one
or two
of you
and
who passionless
prescribes
my passion
and my pain.

Perspective

In your world I am an eagle
carnivorous and sly.
In mine I am small sparrow,
broken-winged, who can not fly.

If You Look For Malice

If you look for malice,
you will find it everywhere, anywhere,
like the old maladies
cured by brown garlic
and old aunts stirring oil
in the alleyways between houses
and two car garages.
My mother taught me
to avoid those harmful hags.
She told me they could ruin any bread,
causing it to become unleavened
out of season.
My mother taught me that malice
is no stranger.
If you look, you will find it anywhere, everywhere.
So I look away and I string my beads
of pain and discontent,
and I hide behind my solitary smile,
and I use my lazy tongue
to wipe away the salivating slights.

Dream

You come from the battlefield.
Your gloryhands red
Like large garden tulips.
I rush to meet you.
My weeping hands white
like winterwashed ravens.

Surreal September, 2001

It is spring, bonfires everywhere,
new green buds sacrificed,
tossed into burning heaps
with last autumn's dead leaves.
The crows are here,
politic as they are,
holding government beneath the stars.
I awaken stunned.

It is late September.
From my window the sky glares too blue.
I carry the dream with me all day.
It does not go away.
Bonfires in my eyes smoke grey.
My brain tries to loose itself from flames.
I pray that in this vast city
there be grace.

Under the Arch

We have walked under columns and through ruins,
Left our shadows trailing, sung toneless tunes
And sought our destinies on cobbled stones
That did not feel our weights.

Hands in pockets to absorb our strengths,
We traveled lightly or heavily, but together.
Braided trees sheltered us, protecting.
And houses in the distance called our names.

And though our youthful bodies bent
to weather storms,
We never looked behind, always beyond.
So has it been with us and so it is.

At One With Lilacs

I crave a lilac tree
wild dark sprays
stroking the crazed corners
of my purpled mind, lapsing now
into mauve memory:
staining clusters curling -
heavy saturating scents
filling the air -
swelling me with pubescent lust,
lulling my brain
to an unseemly perfumed quiet.
And gratifying every part of me,

All I crave is to be one with lilacs.
Then I will rise above myself,
ready to delay the day
and every consequence,
every consequence.

Of Sounds That Would Be Heard

Brain whispers intrude,
Invade this solitude,
Propel this inner force,
Expel this dark remorse
that weighs as albatross.
Brain whispers intrude.
Become as hummingwords
Of sounds that must be heard.
Brain whispers intrude.

Full Circle

If you take a piece of July
and hold it up to a quarter moon,

you will see everything full circle.
It is a law of the seventh month

that keeps us servile to its whims.
There is no way to escape

the flicker of glowworms
and the mounting numbers of summer moths

measuring themselves
against the evening's mourning light.

It is past the year's midway.
We have less than half a year

to catch the calendar.
The glowworms and moths know this.

They depend on us to be unwavering,
to do what we will or what we must.

No Stars Tonight

How can a starless night as this
make wishes made seem promises?

Bitter Herbs

When I have told you,
"I feel no guilt"
You have not believed me.
You have swallowed your grief
Like bitter herbs.
Mine has stuck in my throat
Like some small stone
and for this
I have cursed your silences
and quilted my cares.

On Soundproofing Mind Whispers

There are no words:
only small invasions
into the silences of mind:
small explosions of solitary images

pictures perpendicular to dark spaces:
puzzling pictures hiding
behind lines moving wildly:
no words invited - - no words.

The images cross boundaries
of all remembrances: wire threads
bare themselves against cold bricks
of gold and everything is afire.

There are no words:
everything becomes bold conjuring
and inventive foreplay: lines, shapes,
collages suggestive of nothing
figurative visions: of nothing.
Nothing represents: no signs, no symbols.
Everything limited to unconnectedness -
everything disconnected and disconnecting -

There are no words:
only an absence of thought,
only a prescription for mind smoke.

Arthur Dove at the Heckscher
Centerport

2

A wash of sails
straggles space.
Not enough blue
to curl into.
No comfort cave.
Here fevered yellows flake.
Sharp spokes of orange splice;
and a crewelwork of color
unanticipated,
returns us to an old someplace.

3

This is my home,
a place of tan sun
and blue curves;
waves of upturned hills
stagger the scene.
My pencil - paper-pointed-
confines the chase as
I make of this small rectangle
a place to hide.

Slipping Through Mothersleep

Slipping through night
and mothersleep,
I think of you, dear Mother
and wonder why
we never fortressed ourselves
against the rising tides,
but distanced ourselves instead
from the streams of seasons.
Why did we never learn
to fasten our tears to dreams.
Why did we never learn
to harness silence.
I only learned the restless tricks
that poets play.
I could have learned
the secrets of the stars
and why moons hold us
in their white, white arms . . . .

The Meeting

"Pleased to know you," he said.
I heard the ramblings in his head.
"Pleased to know you," I replied.
And in that instant pleasure died.

Invasions

I know no landscapes
but my own
but
see the hungry eyes,
deep wells of greed,
that steal from inner
landscapes even weed.

Deathfears

Deathfears precipitate a spin
sting mute reminders
that this as All
is not enough for us
who have jagged electrifying storms.
We know the intimidating truth.
There are no hands to break our fall.
No hands at all.

A White, White Day

A torch flares our window,
awakens us.
A storm beginning:

a jeweled eye
falling below horizon,
repeats itself in decibels.

The night has flown from us
offered pink skies.
We quarrel with the gods.

"A white, white day", we cry.
"We want a white, white day."
You hear a whisper, ask me to listen.

I hear it too,
"There is no perfect storm
unless you find perfection in the night."

We close our eyes, return to sleep.

Moon in Mid July

The moon, a giant white pod,
hides behind clouds tonight,
rolls mists of foam,
loses itself in black.
It is strange to see such a moon
in what seemed a monotonous sky,
such a mood-changing
magnetizing moon.

It would take so little
on such a night as this.
to fulfill the prophesy
of lunacy.
How sweet it would be to surrender
every symptom of sanity
for one clear ream
of a ribboning moon
to silvermark this day.

Afterversion: On Viewing Works of The Artist Li Shan

Camel heads cruise canvases,
followed by lump-lean bodies
languishing.
Li Shan's ink dries memory.
Skycrapers, dust atoms now,
are lost in the foam
of the Tien Shen mountains.

We will reinvent ourselves.
This will be a new age
of long journeys
across parching deserts.
Poetry will be born
of cauldron smoke
and these new ashes
will be our monuments.

On "Tangent", 1988
Frankenthaler

I am at tangent with myself
and your splash of greened orange
resonates my landscape.
The black hill at right
is at my left.
As I leave it behind
I squint and find
a blaze of volcanic fire
retched from its bowel.

O, how brazen all of this,
knowing how you despise
interpretation.

Arthur Dove at the Hirschhorn
After Sunrise IV

A cataclysmic orange eye
pupilled in blue,
a cabbage-headed sunrise
not at all true
to all the sunrises
we know or knew.

But squint your eyes
and suddenly the cabbagehead
fights fiercely to free itself
from the surrounding dark,
bleeds to rise again
now and again . . .

Cry Yourself A River

I have seen him turn away
from the dark pools
in your green eyes.
It is not from coldness
but from a heat so red
that it incinerates.
It is best to turn away.
Such fires are never quelled.
Unless one has the courage
for grey ash.

I Wake Up Wet And Sorrowed

Everything is grey and cold, bone-bare.
A silver-coated hag all glazed in white
and twisting knitting needles smiles at me.
I turn aside and move away. A "No"
runs from my mouth and hits the air.
It is no whisper, more like defiant shriek
And then she smiles again,
lips tight and fairy sweet.
Now everything around soft Rembrandt gold.
But for the old hag's hair, a Harlow yellow,
and the grey air overspilling daffodils.
I bend now creeping to a reaching light.
I think I see my mother. Then she's gone.
The old hag grins. I cringe.
What teeth she has are brown.
I crawl away. She pulls my painted hair.
I fall with her into a shallow well
where everything is dark.
I wake up wet and sorrowed.
A fleshy matron humbled in her bed.

Covered Boat 1932
Arthur Dove

I am free
to follow my feet.
The covered boat does not
fence me out.
I am free to step up
to your wheelbarrowed skiff
and laugh at the freedom you give me
to break your rules.

At The Last Moment

You kneeled among the pines
left to dry in this old tomb.
Like Thomas believing
that the end was near,
you touched his wounds.

Were you seeking some sanctuary
to shelter all your cares?
Or did you believe
that you would find forgiveness
if you dared.

Threadbare

The sun spins glaring threads today.
I weave a tapestry.
In spite of skill and sophistry,
the weaving is a shadow-play.

Woman Working At Thai Market
A Mason Sonnet

Thai laughter spills into the tangy air,
Breaking through pungent scents of market day:
Small birds concocted -- fresh with sauces rare --
Readied for sale, and bagged beans red as clay.
The baskets brimmed for labor, not for play,
You shrug your shoulders, shaking off in fun
Whatever burdens life has cast your way.
When market chores are stilled, woman's work done,
What matters most is freedom you have won;
Your journey measured by the selfless role
You have portrayed beneath an eastern sun
That never stained your soul but bronzed your skin
And sturdy hands betraying toothless grin . . . .

My Wife 1941
Arthur Dove

Your wife
a complicated woman
dizzily draped
and enigmatic
    is
like her man
who squares off circles
and circles squares.

Arrangements for Landscapes
Arthur Dove

1

Unboldly but so bravely
this landscape falls into my mindsphere.
Do you see that universal eye
leering at us
as if from amphibian beginning.
Pay no attention to the grey.
It is meant to dilute this space -
to serve as a brief canopy to earth or
a table flat for leaning tree trunks,
or bags of grief.

2

Hills are everywhere in my head.
They elbow my cry for vengeance
among the grappling greens
I colorstitched.
Don't try to corner me.
I've painted myself in.
But if you look closely,
you may see
me walking away
carrying a burden of shapes.

Slipstream

You wander through the slipstream
and I rush past you wandering,
wondering how it is your eyes
are now like hotcoal spheres.

I run from you, the chase too hard,
to search for old, lost slippersocks
like those we dry before the fire
wind-winter nights.

I run to search behind the housedeck
where we left them last. How sad it is
that the night is younger than we,
that there is no time to play

in this cupboarded cold-pantry-world
which we inhabit.
However did this world survive
longer than we, longer than you

who wander through the slipstream,
longer than I who rush from you,
the chase too hard?
How strange it could survive
when we could not.

Zebraed Land

Even fences get lonely.